First Comes Love, Then Comes Marriage 2

THE JOURNEY OF FIRST & SECONDARY VIRGINITY

Ronnesha Butler

Copyright © 2013, 2021. Ronnesha Butler. All rights reserved.
Unless otherwise indicated, scriptures are taken from The English Standard Version Holy Bible © 2002 by Crossway bibles.

www.Ronneshasjournal.com

Book Layout ©2013 BookDesignTemplates.com

Quantity sales and special discounts are available. *For details* *Email:* Ronneshasbooks@gmail.com

First Comes Love, Then Comes Marriage II -- 1st ed.
ISBN-13: 978-1481806107
ISBN-10: 1481806106

Dear Reader,

Although I was encouraged to, I never thought I would write a book on first and secondary virginity. I originally wrote a book on abstinence almost two years ago, but I couldn't imagine writing anything else about abstinence. But God laid on my heart six months later to write this book, and suddenly *First Comes Love, Then Comes Marriage* felt unfinished. He began to give me chapter by chapter, and I am excited to share it with you. This book was written for those who are needing encouragement in their journey with Christ as well as their journey of sexual purity.

I hope that this book will assist you in your journey.

–Ronnesha

Dear Reader,

I wrote this book in 2013. Today as I revisit this book, it is 2022. In June of 2021, I began to feel a tug and a restlessness that I could not explain. I have never had an issue with sleeping, so it was strange to me that I was unusually restless and unsettled. After a couple of weeks of this, I did something I should have done in the beginning. I prayed about it. After praying and asking God the reason I was feeling unsettled, He brought me back to this book that I neglected over the years. Almost 10 years to be exact.

"For such a time as this." That was the verse and message I kept hearing concerning this book. We know the story of Esther and how Esther had a specific assignment for her people that was "For such a time as this." I wrote this book you are holding in your hand nine years ago, and when I felt the tug to revamp this book, I was surprised but I understood why. This wasn't a popular message back when I wrote it in 2013, and it is even less popular today, but it is a message I believe God has called me to teach for such a time as this. Such a time as this where God's design for sex and sexuality has been perverted and conformed to fit the narrative of the culture. For such a time as this where it seems anything goes. For such a time as this, where the current and next generation is being bombarded with messages and agendas. So although I never thought I would revise or relaunch this book, I couldn't deny that I was called to do it.

So here I am...writing again. Feeling the assignment was unfinished...again. At first, I asked myself "What is the use of writing this book in a culture that seems so Anti-Christ?". But I realize that in the darkness, the light shines and that is the moment God needs His servants to bring light and His message to the dark places. There are still people who love God. There are still people who desire righteousness. There are still people who are not conformed to this world. There is still a remnant in this generation. There is still an assignment and responsibility for us to speak what God's Word says regardless of what time and day we are living in. I remind myself of that, and I remind you of that as well. Enjoy this book and I pray it helps you as much as it has helped me and others in the past. This book is still in its original message from 2013 except for a few added sections such as this one but it is still the same message that never changes. I must insert a disclosure here. This is not a sex education book. It's not that I don't think sex education is not important, but this is not the purpose of this book. In this book, you will not find any information on STDs, teen pregnancy, or abortion statistics nor am I trying to sway anyone or preach to anyone in this book. Instead, this book is what I feel God has laid on my heart as a way of encouragement and teaching on a topic that I believe the Lord has placed inside of me and tugged on me to relaunch.... for such a time as this.

-Ronnesha

Thank You

To my parents and family for their encouragement in writing this book.

To my pastor and church family for their constant support since 2011.

To the readers and youth leaders who have taken the time to read this book.

To the Lord for giving me an opportunity to live for Him.

At 19 years old, I am living in a society that tries to convince me that abstinence is a thing of the past. I took the pledge to remain abstinent in high school, but for no other reason besides avoiding pregnancy. Yeah, I know abstinence is the right way to go, but it's too vague for me. The world has given me plenty of reasons why I shouldn't wait to have sex, but no one explains to me why I should abstain from sex until I am married besides the obvious fact that God created sex for marriage. I am told I should be exploring and indulging in things that satisfy my flesh. They tell me everyone is doing it and abstinence is an old fashion practice. They also tell me that it is a stress reliever. Stress is huge in my life at this age of coming to know who I am and what I want in life. They even tell me I don't need to have a commitment. If I make the decision to not wait until marriage, the world will tell me how. They offer condoms, birth control, and other methods to avoid getting "caught." How come after I take the pledge to remain abstinent no one tells me where to go from there? Where are the other 19-year old's that are abstaining? How do I fight this temptation? I have a boyfriend now, should we be alone like this? I took the pledge now what? Forget it. I want things to make sense.

At 23 years old, I still live in that society. The society that continuously tries to convince me that I have made an unrealistic decision to remain abstinent. I am still told that I should be indulging in things that satisfy my flesh. I should be living it up in my 20's. I don't want to say that since I am a believer it is easy because that is far from the truth. I still sometimes battle with the thoughts I had at 19 years old. Society still tries to pamper my conviction with remedies by telling me how to have safe sex. I found out three years ago that there is no such thing as safe sex. No one told me what to do when "safe sex" turned out to be a life changer for me. Let's not even start with the emotional effects I dealt with. I didn't get pregnant or catch an STD, but I hurt emotionally, and society wasn't there for me. My family and God had to reconstruct my feelings that you destroyed. You didn't tell me about the guilt and condemnation that almost took everything from me. You didn't tell me how far I would feel from God. But I have learned from the past, and your deception. I have learned that the enemy encourages me to sin, then condemns me. Oh yeah... and not everyone is doing it. There are people my age who are abstaining too. Who would have thought? I made the decision to allow the Holy Spirit to guide my heart and will for a reason.

Contents

Sex is Good.
Introduction
PART ONE: To Not Conform
PART TWO: Using Your Tools
PART THREE: Flesh versus Spirit
Condemnation
Temptation
Ways to Fight Temptation
Sanctification
The "S" Season
Conclusion

Sex is Good

Sex is good. Let me say that again... sex is good. Sex is good because God created sex. Sex was not created by Hollywood, television, magazines, nor movies, but GOD created sex. God created sex as a gift for our enjoyment, and pleasure, to be fruitful and multiply our families and the earth, and to bring glory to Him in the covenant of marriage.

I understand that "Purity Culture" in the past had gained a reputation that was not so good because some forms of teaching, did not reiterate the fact that sex is indeed good. So as a result, some women (and some men) experienced feeling "yucky" or guilty on their wedding night when this shouldn't be. Sex is not "yucky" or unnatural it is just designed to be enjoyed in the way God intended on it to be enjoyed... within the marriage covenant. There were mistakes in the purity culture that people do not mind pointing out and criticizing. Nevertheless, God's standard is still right. Once we understand that Sexual sin has consequences whether that be physical, spiritual, emotional, or even at times financial we understand why sex is designed the way it is. In Biblical stories, we find cities being destroyed and individuals in the Bible chastised and judged because of sexual sin. But also, today we see the consequences of sex used out of context. We see perversion out of control, hardened hearts, divorce caused by adultery, and not to mention all the social problems that have been the cause of debates and division. As a sociology major, I am amazed at how much God's Word intertwines and validates the root of social issues. God created sex, and we as human beings cannot change His design for it no matter what the times say, or what the year is. You may understand and know firsthand from experience the consequences of sexual sin, but the good news is that we have a God that says, "Your sins are forgiven, go and sin no more." We have a God that makes garments to cover us after disobeying and entering a zone of crossing over the boundaries God put in place as He did for Adam and Eve after the fall. And although Adam and Eve had to walk out of the garden, in consequence, they walked out covered with God's provision of animal skin over their naked bodies as a reminder of God's forgiveness and grace. So be encouraged and not ashamed if this is you. We have a God full of mercy and redemption.

Introduction

I made the decision to abstain from sex until marriage in September 2010. This is an eight-month difference between the time I received salvation and the time I made this decision. Yes, that is upside down considering that's a whole eight months. I didn't make a full out decision to walk out God's design for sex as a standard and commitment to Christ. Why not? Well, I was not only spiritually bankrupt, but I was also biblically ignorant. I knew premarital sex was wrong, but because of the: people I spent most of my time with, my personal views on sex at the time (I used to think people were just being religious when they told you about no sex before marriage), and because I allowed society to shape my mentality, I thought it was harmless. I had no discipleship at the time or anyone who could pull me to the side to explain to me both the importance and the requirement of dying to your flesh after you are born again. I had no idea that I had to allow the Lord to change my mentality to His mentality. So, I made the decision; great! But then came opposition. Now I was both confused and discouraged because I realized that I could not carry this out on my own. There were new temptations and distractions I had no clue about.

You make the decision to live a set apart life, but then opposition comes to try to do everything it can to interrupt your decision. Typical. Opposition then tries everything from discouragement to temptation to have you turn away from your commitment to live a life for Christ (and this isn't just pertaining to sex). Typical. That opposition is normal because it becomes more than a decision you make; it becomes a war between your flesh and spirit.

If you have made the decision to live a life according to God's ways, and you have faced difficulty along with that decision, I know exactly how you feel because I was only 20 years old when I made the decision, and I am 23 years old now. So, there were times after I made the decision when I was so tempted that I almost gave in, and I didn't think I would be able to continue with not only purity, but the Christian life.

I know how it is being at the age where sin is almost encouraged because you have this newfound freedom. Not only do I understand, but Jesus understands too. He knows the pressure you deal with daily; He knows the things that try to hinder your spiritual growth, but He has given you tools to fight temptation or whatever opposition that attempts to come against you and me. He has also given us His Holy Spirit to guide us through our entire walk with Christ. If you have found that you have certain difficulties in this journey continue to read.

PART ONE
To Not Conform

I appeal to you therefore, brothers by the mercies of God, to present your bodies as a living sacrifice, holy and acceptable to God which is your spiritual worship. Do not be conformed to this world but be transformed by the renewal of your mind, that by testing you may discern what is the will of God, what is good and acceptable and perfect. -**Romans 12:1-2**

According to Merriam Webster dictionary, *conform* means "to be similar or identical; to be in agreement or harmony; and to be obedient or compliant." *Conform* also means "to act in accordance with prevailing standards or customs."[1]

In Romans 12:1-2, Paul urged the Romans not to conform to the world and it's obvious that the same goes for us today. But what does that mean? This means that we are not to be similar, identical, in agreement, nor accepting of the standards of the world—including the world's view of sex.

Sex (world's view) = No limits. No boundaries. Do as your flesh is willing. Abstinence is unrealistic.

Sex (God's view) = Sacred. Designed for marriage. Realistic with the assistance of the Holy Spirit.

---

[1] "conform." *Merriam-Webster.com*. Merriam-Webster, 2011. Web. 1 Feb. 2013

We must put our personal opinions aside and our culture aside and put our trust in the word of God as the ultimate truth because we have died to our old selves, opinions, and pre-Christ thoughts, and we are now alive in Him once we are born again. Although abstinence is mentioned in the world, it is not viewed in the same way believers view abstinence. To the world, abstinence is a preventative plan that is the only assured way to prevent STDs and pregnancy. Abstinence is not encouraged to live a righteous life, but to protect you from physical consequences. We cannot deny the physical benefits of abstaining from premarital sex as well as emotional benefits, but our primary motivation for abstinence as believers should be righteousness and holiness. And it's never too late to start over again. I started out with the viewpoint of the world pertaining to abstinence by thinking it was "old-fashioned." But when I made the decision that I was going to strive to live following Christ and no longer conform to the world, I came up with a few reasons why.

Reason 1

It is God's will for me to abstain from pre-marital sex.

For this is the will of God, your sanctification. That you abstain from sexual immorality; that each one of you knows how to control his/her own body.

1 Thessalonians 4:3-4

A local radio show host asked me one day, "What would you say to girls who have no father figure?" I responded, "Understand that God is a father." One of the first things I came to know about the Lord is that He is not only a father, but a good father, and a good father prohibits you from doing things that will cause you harm. A good father lays out boundaries to protect his children, and although their children may not see the harm in what he has forbidden them to do; he sees the harm clearly and strives to protect them.

The other day my seven-month-old nephew was trying to grab the iron while I was ironing, and with me knowing the harm it would do to him, I wouldn't allow him to touch it. He didn't like that I was keeping him from playing with the iron, so he started to cry. But I knew I was protecting him from being burned. I am obviously not a father, but the same way I tried to protect my nephew, the Lord does for us. He lays His will out for us to follow to prevent us from being hurt. He doesn't lay boundaries to keep us from "living life to the fullest." But the opposite is true. He does want us to live life to the fullest, but not the way the world defines living. He wants us to live eternally with Him. He wants us to live a righteous life. He wants us to avoid unnecessary heartache. We may not see the importance of His will at first, but we will eventually see the importance.

Read: I Thessalonians 4:3-4. What does that scripture mean to you?

_____
_____
_____
_____
_____
_____

Why do you think God has laid out standards for us to follow?

_____
_____
_____
_____
_____
_____

Read: Romans 12:1-2. What does conforming to this world mean to you?

_____
_____
_____
_____
_____
_____
_____

What are some qualities that God has that has directly affected your life one or more times? (Ex: God as a healer after healing your body)

_____
_____
_____
_____
_____

Reason 2
It is the enemy's desire to see us fall

Be sober-minded; be watchful. Your adversary the devil prowls around like a roaring lion, seeking someone to devour.

I Peter 5:8

I once heard a preacher say, "The picture Satan is painting is not as beautiful as it looks. If you can see beyond the canvas, you will see pain, shame, and humiliation." What a powerful and true statement. My parents were heavily involved in ministry while I was growing up, so I was required to always attend church. Because of that upbringing, I used to feel as if I was missing out on things other people my age were doing. I couldn't attend middle or high school parties that were thrown for teenagers my age, and I couldn't listen to secular music. Those two things were big deals during high school, and I felt like a misfit while others talked about the things that took place at the latest party. Cut to four years later when I moved out on my own and started my first year of college. I began to dabble in sin, but it wasn't sinning to me, it was "newfound freedom." Little did I know that "newfound freedom" would soon become bondage because I felt chained by the pleasure of wanting to continue in sin. I was attracted to bondage with real consequences and a real price tag (Romans 6:23. Galatians 6:8). The enemy wants to see us all disobey the Lord and see us fall in the process. So, he offers things that lead us to sin, which in turn offers destruction because you can be sure anything that he offers us will have the intent of destructing us or separating us from the benefits of living life the way God intends for us to live it. (Genesis 3)

Read: I Peter 5:8. What does that scripture mean to you?

_____
_____
_____
_____
_____
_____

Why does the enemy want us to disobey God's design & will?

_____
_____
_____
_____
_____
_____

Random: How does the kind of music I listen to have an impact on me and my spiritual walk with Christ?

_____
_____
_____
_____
_____
_____

Reason 3
My body is a temple

Flee from sexual immorality. Every other sin a person commits is outside of the body, but the sexually immoral person sins against his own body. Do you know that your body is a temple of the Holy Spirit within you, whom you have from God? For you were bought with a price. So, glorify God in your body.

1 Corinthians 6:18-20

First Comes Love, Then Comes Marriage

Read: I Corinthians 6:18-20. What does this scripture mean to me?

_____
_____
_____
_____
_____

How can I glorify God with my body?

_____
_____
_____
_____
_____
_____
_____

How was I bought with a price?

_____
_____
_____
_____
_____

Reason 4

Sex is meant for the covenant of marriage, which protects me from unhealthy emotional attachments and ties. (Genesis 2:24)

The bond that comes from sexual intercourse was meant to be so powerful that it binds a couple together as "one flesh" for the rest of their lives. When a person participates in sex before marriage, they allow themselves to have the same bond with that person. In 1 Corinthians 6:13, Paul made it clear to the Corinthian people that sexual immorality was not meant for the body, but the body meant for the Lord. Then Paul goes a little more in-depth in 1 Corinthians 6:16 saying,

"Do you not know that he who is joined to a prostitute becomes one body with her? For it is written, 'the two will become one flesh.'"

That is what some call having a "soul tie". There has been debate about the word as to whether it is biblical but let us go to a practical level that many of us know is true. Sex does bring emotional attachments. It was designed to because it is designed to create a bond to last during the covenant union of marriage. That is one of the reasons why having sex is so important inside of marriage and can be damaging outside of marriage. On a scientific level, sex releases the hormone oxytocin which is the same hormone that is released during childbirth and nursing. So, for women oxytocin creates a strong bonding. Because of this, it is hard for some people especially women to leave relationships that they know are not God's best or are toxic in nature because they have already bonded on such a high level with this person. It is almost a ripping when breaking up and can be very emotional and hard because you have shared your vessel on this earth (aka your body) with this person. So, whether people believe in "Soul Ties" per se, we can agree that there are indeed emotional bonds that are created during sex.

For the sake of this book, I am going to refer to these attachments as "ties". The Bible does reference ungodly and godly ties though. I personally believe that Samson had an unhealthy tie with Delilah. When people say "Soul ties" of course we are not saying your soul is lost, but your soul is made of your mind, will, and emotions, and a tie represents being joined. When your mind, will, and emotions are joined to someone else it can cause deep hurt when betrayed, making it hard to part with a person even if the relationship has been over for some time. "Soul ties" bring the emotional consequences of premarital sex, and it can be a hurtful experience. Even those who do not believe in the Bible, have attested to the fact that sex is not just a physical act but impacts a person's spiritual, physical, and emotional realm. The Word of God also says sex is the only sin that sins directly against the body (I Corinthians 6:18).

Struggling with an Unhealthy Attachment?

There are some of you reading who may be still dealing with the emotional impacts of sexual experiences before marriage or even traumatic experiences that were not your fault pertaining to sex. These impacts can be so traumatizing that they can impact and affect almost every area of your life if not dealt with and healed. Just as a heads up, this next paragraph or two may be a trigger alert to those who may have dealt with sexual abuse in the past.

If you were violated by someone who misused sex against you, I am in NO WAY saying that you have sinned. No! You were sinned against and you most likely are carrying trauma, and that trauma is very real. I am so sorry that happened to you and I pray that you experience complete and total inner healing from it. I believe that "Purity Culture" in the past has hurt many victims of sexual abuse by telling them that they were in some ways "dirty" because of something that happened to them. That they are not "pure" because of something that was done against them, and that is very harmful, toxic, and is not the heart of the Father. If that was you in the past and you have not dealt with that trauma in your life, I want to encourage you to seek the help you need with a good therapist that can help you navigate, process, and begin the process of healing from that trauma. I personally recommend a good therapist that you feel comfortable with that can help you navigate this season of healing. I also had to go through a season of healing and therapy for a totally different issue, but that issue although not sexual abuse was extremely harmful to my mental, emotional, and spiritual health. The reason I have always chosen Christian therapists over others is that trauma has a way of impacting your view of God and I needed to have that qualified Christian therapist who has the Holy Spirit indwelling in them to point me back to the ultimate healer and remove that feeling of "Where was God?" and making Him the enemy and perpetrator. Does that make sense?

Yes, the trauma may be very real, but the good news is we have a very real God that can heal us from any emotional pain, wound, broken heart, trauma, or experience that seems like it can never be healed. He can heal us and make us testimonies and an agent of healing for others who are hurting. Therapy is a resource of healing, but it is not the ultimate source. God is the ultimate source of our healing. Now back to those of us who fell short and sinned.

His Word says that if we confess our sin, He is faithful and just to not only forgive us for the sin but cleanse us. We serve a good Father who gives good gifts to His children and one of those gifts is healing our emotional wounds and hurts. If your heart is still broken, He heals broken hearts. If you are still wounded, He binds up your wounds. Go ahead, get with Him, and pour out that hurt on Him. He will give you rest, and He heals. I believe any attachment, any situation, any emotional bondage can be broken by the power of God. Cry out to Him. Be honest with Him. Watch Him work.

My favorite part of 1 Corinthians 6 is verse 17 where it makes it clear that if you are joined to the Lord, you will become one spirit with Him. Seek His face and continue to pray that He not only breaks the emotional attachment but that you can experience being one spirit with Him. But you have work to do as well. When I was struggling with an unhealthy emotional attachment, I had to reject anything that reminded me of the person and our former relationship. I had to stop replaying memories of days spent together and rehearsing conversations we had. I had to throw away gifts that were given and delete those text messages I wanted so badly to keep just so I could reread them.

Read: Genesis 2:24. What does this scripture mean to you?

_____
_____
_____
_____
_____
_____

Reason 5
I have a calling as a child of God

Flee also youthful lusts: but follow righteousness, faith, charity, peace, with them that call on the Lord out of a pure heart.

2 Timothy 2:22

I believe we all have a calling from God on our lives that brings Him glory. We have the calling to die to ourselves and pursue righteousness and to love the Lord God with all our hearts, ourselves, and others. But I also believe we have individual assignments that God has for us to do while on this earth. In other words, I don't believe God forms you in your mother's womb without a purpose. I went on my first fast in February 2010. During this fast, I dedicated my future to Christ and found out what it was that God had assigned me to do on this earth for Him. I told God, "Whatever it is you want me to do or say in this lifetime, please let me know and I will do it. I know this doesn't end with receiving salvation, so what do you want from me?"

First, He showed me that He wants me to love Him with all my heart. Then He revived a passion I had for years. I have kept a journal since I was eleven years old, and I keep one to this day. So, from the time I was eleven years old, anytime something exciting, sad, or life-changing happened, I wrote about it. I even wrote when nothing happened that day because I just loved to express myself through writing. It was my passion.

I eventually started journaling my life with Christ. While journaling one day, He began to give me burdens for people that He wanted me to write to. He wanted me to focus on writing for young women who were going through depression; self-esteem issues, brokenhearted, and lost. All I had to do was ask Him what He created me for and make the sacrifice to find out, and He revealed it to me. I told the Lord one night that I didn't want to just make it to heaven, but I want Him to look at me and say, "Well done." I want to fulfill what He wants me to fulfill for Him and do it well. Spend time with Him and find out what you can do for His kingdom while on earth. When you find out, don't allow sin to corrupt your assignment nor the world to pervert the gift God has given you.

You even must protect yourself from condemnation attempting to ruin your life and destiny. A lot of times we allow our past and our mistakes to come in between the assignment God has given us, even after we have repented. I went through a phase of condemnation coming close to ruining my assignment. I felt like I wasn't good enough or qualified for the assignment God had given me because of things that I faced in my life. I felt like I had failed God, and I wanted Him to pick someone else to do my assignment for me. But God can take our past condemnation and turn it into a testimony for others that may be going through the same things we are going through now. If I never would have pushed past that condemnation and guilt, you wouldn't be reading this book today.

One of the oldest tricks in the book from Satan is to send wicked relationships into the lives of God's children. One example is Samson in the Bible. Samson was set apart by God and given a supernatural strength. When Samson was conceived, his mother was barren and couldn't have children and the angel of the lord brought news that she would conceive a son. Obviously, when an angel of the Lord comes and gives news of a miraculous birth, the child has a unique calling from the Lord. Many times, the Spirit of the Lord came upon Samson, and this brought on a supernatural strength. The Philistines couldn't defeat him, but they knew he had fallen in love with a woman named Delilah, so they offered her some money to find the secret to Samson's strength. Eventually after telling Delilah lies about his strength, he told her the truth. I still don't understand how after it was obvious that she was asking to set him up, he still gave her his secret. Anyhow, in the end, the philistines gauged Samson's eyes out after shaving off his hair. But his hair began to grow back. It may have been a little peach fuzz, but it grew back. When he was brought to entertain them, Samson called out to God and made some requests. In the end, Samson ended up killing more people on that day than he did all his life. The strength left Samson the moment he cut his hair which was the key to his strength and one of the instructions given by God. He disobeyed God and not only did the spirit of the Lord leave him, but he ended up blind with gauged-out eyes. In the end, God ended up in His grace allowing Samson to kill more in one day than in his whole life. We all have a calling from God, and "love" if wrong and not orchestrated by God, can become a downfall. Ask me how I know. I don't recall reading in the story anywhere where Samson was relying on the strength giver. But you notice once Samson began to call out to God, he accomplished more at that moment than in his whole life with a full head of hair and eyesight. We may get ourselves in a mess or a bind by disobeying God which can impact our lives, but we have a God of grace who tells us in His word if we confess our sins, He is faithful to not only forgive us but cleanse us. (I John 1:9) God can still use us in a place of shame or failure.

Read 2 Timothy 2:22. How does this scripture pertain to my calling as a child of God?

_____
_____
_____
_____
_____
_____
_____
_____
_____

Do I know what my assignment is from God? Do I know my purpose?

_____

What is it? (If yes)

_____
_____
_____
_____

First Comes Love, Then Comes Marriage

_____
_____

Do I allow the Lord to guide me in doing what He has called me to do in this life?

_____
_____

What are my goals?

_____
_____
_____
_____
_____

Do I pray about those goals to make sure it is what God wants me to pursue?

_____
_____
_____
_____

PART TWO

Using Your Tools

At the 2003 annual meeting of the American Psychological Society, researchers reported that over 60% of college students who had pledged virginity during their middle or high school years had broken their vow to remain abstinent until marriage

We live in a sexually saturated culture where premarital sex is acceptable, schools are replacing abstinence-only programs with safe sex education, celebrities who are also role models for young girls are promoting sex, and the temptation to participate is weighing on those who may have a desire to abstain. In the last chapter, I shared a few reasons I have chosen to abstain. Even with the increase of abstinence pledges being broken according to statistics, I don't think pledges, in general, are ineffective, I think the intention for pledging is what makes it ineffective. Sometimes it is easy to make an abstinence pledge because it is a part of a program or service, not because you intend to live it out. I believe in pledges, but I feel it is more genuine when it is a commitment done between a person and God. A year and a half ago, I made the pledge below to the Lord.

"I am making a commitment to God to abstain until marriage. I realize that sex before marriage is just the trap the enemy has brought to pervert the perfect gift God created between husbands and wives. I commit myself as I allow the Holy Spirit to help me in any weak area that I may have. I commit to participate in the transformation process so as I strive to live this life of purity I will remember to depend on the word of God as my shield and lamp. I will throw off any and everything that hinders and the sin that so easily entangles and run with perseverance the race marked out as it tells me in Hebrews 12:1. I will aspire to live as a true echo of Christ no matter what I have done in the past. I decide today to follow your Word so that I can strive for holiness this day forward!"

I typed that pledge on paper, decorated it, and printed it out to sign. It wasn't some requirement or stamp of my decision; I just felt led to do it. It is more important that it is written in your heart.

Feel free to write your own commitment to the Lord if that is what you feel. It doesn't have to be perfect or "well written," it just needs to come from your heart.

Tool 1
Don't rely on your own strength

When we try to live a holy lifestyle on our own instead of relying on the Holy Spirit and the Word of God to guide us, we fail. The flesh can't fight against the flesh; the spirit must dominate over it until it dies. The Holy Spirit is our helper (John 14:26), and the Word is our guide (Psalm 119:105). So, when we are trying to live for Christ, we have to receive help from the Holy Spirit and put the Word of God as a priority. Growing up, I didn't understand the Bible. It wasn't until I started to read, meditate, and obey it that I started to see the transformation take place and realized that is only by the work of the Holy Spirit. When I was first born again, I allowed my relationship with Christ to substitute for reading the Bible. I came to know Christ from a hurting place, so to me, He was a healer and a friend only. Then I was at a place where my relationship with Him became stagnant. Not because I wasn't fellowshipping with Him, but because I knew Him as nothing else. I didn't know His attributes, His character, how He reacted to His children, what He required, how He prayed, His will, or how He lived. I knew He died for our sins, but I never knew the depth of what that really meant until I started to read the Bible. I now look at the Bible as the actual words of God on paper that are available to me, and I can read what He says and grow in a deeper knowledge of who He is. So, in this journey, it is important to make sure to invest in the Word of God daily

Do I lean on my own strength or the Lord's strength?

Read John 14. Think about what this chapter means to you.

_____
_____
_____
_____
_____
_____
_____
_____
_____

What are some ways the Holy Spirit is my helper?

_____
_____
_____
_____
_____
_____
_____
_____
_____

Tool 2
Relationship with Christ

Do you know that Jesus wants us to have a personal relationship with Him? He wants us to seek Him and find out what it is He made us for so that we can serve Him mightily in the Kingdom of God. He also wants to transform us. So, the Holy Spirit convicts us of sin so that we can be transformed and separated from the world. The Lord loves us with a love deeper than anyone can comprehend or display to us. I am amazed at how He wants to talk to and guide us. I love how I can get in my car and just ride and talk to Him about anything and know that He is literally listening to every word. I can go from stress to total peace after spending time talking to Him and reading His word. He is truly my best friend.

But there was a time I struggled with keeping a relationship with the Lord. I would get bored in His presence and would feel tempted to pick up my phone instead of my Bible in the mornings. I wasn't satisfied with my relationship with the Lord, so I came up with what I call "The Spiritual Exercise" and did this for 30 days straight.

The Spiritual Exercise

1. I found a quiet place.
2. When I spent time with the Lord, I cut out all distractions. This could mean leaving a phone or a laptop in another room during quiet time.
3. I didn't spend my entire prayer time praying solely about myself but spent time praying for His will and other people as well.
4. I carved out a specified time of the day to spend unrushed time with the Lord.

On a scale from 1-10 my relationship with Christ is a ___

When was the last time I spent time with God?

Do I believe God wants to spend time with me?

If not, why not?

_____
_____
_____
_____
_____
_____

If yes, why?

_____
_____
_____
_____
_____

TOOL 3
Accountability

When I first became born again, I had more people around me that tore me down in the faith than built me up, and that kind of damaged my walk with Christ in the beginning. That is why I believe it is important to have some type of accountability in your life. Whether that is from attending weekly Bible studies with other believers or having an actual mentor to assist you with the Christian walk. Those early relationships were destroying me so badly, that I prayed that God would help me find a new job with less worldly influence. I even prayed for God to temporarily remove me and my then-best friend's relationship without hurting her feelings. I believe it was a prayer that God honored because He answered the prayer a month later. I could handle the atmosphere and people now, but at the time I didn't need those kinds of influences in my life at such an early stage of salvation.

If you don't have any accountability right now, I would pray about it. I didn't have a church home for a period and was not surrounded by young Christians who I could grow in Christ with, and trust to hold me accountable. But I had the desire to have both. So, I prayed, asking God to help me find a church home that would help me grow in Him and hold me accountable and He did almost a week later.

One of the main complaints from young or new Christians is not having young radical Christian friends, and that can make the Christian walk lonely. Not only that, but it can cause young Christians to go back to old habits with old friends for the sake of fellowship. It was crucial for me that I didn't purposely expose myself to a lot of people who believed it was cool to live in sin even if that meant being alone for a season or two. I invested time in reading blogs of young adults who were striving to live for God, and I would read testimonies of young adults who were going through the same things I was going through as a baby Christian.

Sometimes we run from accountability because we don't want anyone "in our business," or "judging us." But it should be an honor to have people who care enough about your life to keep you accountable. Remember that God put accountability in place for us to protect us.

Are my friends more of a hindrance to my walk with God or do they help me become closer to Him?

_____
_____
_____
_____

PART THREE
Flesh Vs Spirit

For the desires of the flesh are against the spirit and the desires of the spirit are against the flesh, for these are opposed to each other to keep you from doing the things you want to do.

Galatians 5:17

There are two desires, the flesh, and the spirit, and they are warring against each other constantly until the flesh is put to death. That is why we can desire what we know is wrong, but at the same time have the conviction to not go feed that desire. It is the war between your flesh and spirit. What if you have remained a virgin, but now the temptation is whispering for you to participate in sex before marriage? What if you have been dealing with lustful thinking? What do you do in this war? What if condemnation from the past is too heavy? How do you allow the spirit to win? Starve the flesh. Let's look at two major flesh wars that try to hold you back when you are trying to abstain: **condemnation** and **temptation**.

Condemnation

There is therefore now no condemnation to those who are in Christ Jesus who do not walk according to the flesh, but according to the Spirit. (KJV)

Romans 8:1

As I shared earlier, I remember experiencing strong condemnation after realizing that I had an emotional attachment with my ex-boyfriend. We had been broken up for almost two years and I was a born-again Christian now. I was walking down the whole strip of a street going to my car, embarrassed to look people in the eye because I didn't want them to see my tears. When I finally got home to my bedroom, I cried nonstop. As I was crying, I repented and asked God to forgive me for participating in His gift to married couples before it was time. I also asked Him to take away any emotional attachment that I had with that person. After praying that prayer, I was reminded of Romans 8:1.

Because I repented, was forgiven, and no longer walked according to the flesh, I felt condemnation break off me. You may have already participated in premarital sex and are currently experiencing an emotional tie but couldn't explain what it was. The first thing is repentance. Then make it a part of your lifestyle to walk according to the spirit from now on. To make sure of that, you must continue to keep a relationship with Christ. You may not immediately feel changed, but the transformation is a process.

Continue to pray in the expectation that you will see the fruit of the heartfelt prayer you prayed to God concerning that bond you created with that person. First Thessalonians 5:7 has been a key Scripture in my prayer life. There are certain things I had been praying for over a year, and since it was according to His will, it was answered.

Do you know how hard it is to wait for God to answer a prayer you know is His will for over a year? Very hard for me; but I had to trust that in His timing it would be answered, and it was. No matter how bound you feel to a certain thing, if you know you are praying for God's will, then trust that you will not struggle with bondage or condemnation for the rest of your life.

I believe condemnation is one of the enemy's main tools to keep you from going forward in your walk with Christ. You may have made bad decisions, but once you repent with a sincere heart to walk by the spirit from then on; there is no condemnation for you. I used to feel as David described in Psalm 38:3 when he said, "There is no health in my bones because of my sin." But God continued to show me I was forgiven no matter what I had done. I prayed this prayer to God:

I believe in the power of your shed blood, and because of that power I believe there is no condemnation for me because I am in you, and I don't walk according to the flesh but by the spirit. So, there is no way I can hold on to this condemnation. My sin is washed away.

I no longer saw filth but saw my sins covered in the blood of Jesus washing away every shameful thing from my past. I saw myself freed from condemnation.

Do I constantly feel condemned about past mistakes?
_____
_____

If so, recite Romans 8:1

Do I believe that God wants me to feel condemned about my past?
_____
_____
_____
_____
_____
_____

Temptation

When I used to think about temptation, the word *failure* came to mind. Now when I think about temptation, I think about "the exit." We talk about the entry door—which is how you got in the place to be tempted—but we hardly talk about the exit door that has been provided for us. In every situation where temptation is present, we have a way of escape. First Corinthians 10:13 says:

There hath no temptation taken you, but such as is common to man: but God is faithful, who will not suffer you to be tempted above that ye are able; but will with the temptation also make a way to escape, that ye may be able to bear it.

First Comes Love, Then Comes Marriage

There were plenty of times I had to use the exit door in other areas of my life, but one specific time where I had to use the exit door was with a guy, whom I will call Bob. A little bit after I got saved, Bob—a guy I had known for almost 10 years—asked me out on a date. After our date, we grew even closer as friends, and Bob and I developed a crush on each other. We wanted to be in a more serious relationship, but because we lived in different states it wasn't reasonable right then. So, we made plans that once we both lived in the same state again, we would become a couple.

One problem with that was that I continued to get convicted of the plan of our relationship. Our original plan was to move in together, and then get married. Although that is normal in society, it wasn't a standard God approved of because that would open us up to tempting situations. I used to think if I moved in God will test me, but I was an infant Christian and now I know that wouldn't have been a test; it would have been a tempting situation that I put myself in. One night I studied the way Jesus handled temptation. I read Matthew 4 probably three times that night.

Temptation

- ☐ Its intention is to bring you further away from Christ.
- ☐ Temptation pulls on you to disobey the Word of God.
- ☐ Giving in to temptation brings shame, dishonor, sin, and destruction.

Adam and Eve giving in to temptation remains a prime example of being overcome by temptation. (Genesis 3)

Test

- ☐ Its intention is to bring you closer to the Lord.
- ☐ A test gives you an opportunity to follow the Word of God.
- ☐ Passing a test or enduring temptation brings honor and a reward. (James 1:3, 12)

First Comes Love, Then Comes Marriage

Bob was a temptation, not a test, so I had to take the exit door. My exit door was cutting off any communication that would lead to giving Bob the wrong impression of our relationship status. I knew this was not a person I could see myself marrying because he didn't have the Godly attributes described in the Bible. I no longer put him under the impression that we were anything more than friends. I even sent him a long message telling him that because our paths were different, we could no longer have the relationship we had before or planned to have because I needed someone that would push me closer to Christ, not further away from Him. He is a nice guy, so he commended my stand and assured me that he would never want to stand in the way of my relationship with Christ. I'm not going to say it was easy to just cut off contact with someone I had grown close to, but it was necessary for me because I didn't want to waste his time or mine. Was our relationship bad? Not really, but it had the potential to draw me off the path I knew I was called to walk.

The Lord wasn't putting me in tempting situations; I was putting myself in tempting situations when I listened to my flesh by putting myself in a position I knew I shouldn't have been in. My exit door was saying, "No, this is not the path I am to walk so I am leaving this path now." Remember that we always have an exit door.

Ways to Fight Temptation

1.   **Read the Word of God.** Not only does reading the Word of God tell us how to overcome, but it also shows the consequences of sin and giving into temptation.

2.   **Recognize a ploy of destruction.** When you see Satan as someone who offers destruction no matter how good it looks, it changes your perception of sin.

3.   **Take the exit door.** Whether that door is an actual door or cutting off communication, you have an exit door available to you. (1 Corinthians 10:13)

4.   **Pray and watch for potential traps.** Read Luke 22:46

5.   **See the armor of God as your protection in battle.** (Ephesians 6:10-17)

Read Matthew 4:1-11

What are some ways that we fight temptation?

_____
_____
_____
_____

How did Jesus's handle temptation?

_____
_____
_____
_____
_____

Explain the exit?

_____
_____
_____
_____
_____
_____

PART FOUR
Sanctification

Simply put, *sanctification* is "being set apart for a specific purpose to be made holy."

Not only is sanctification an important transformation after salvation, but if I had at least half of the knowledge about sanctification that I have now, it would have saved me a lot of confusion, discouragement, and complaining. Before I understood the process and purpose of sanctification, I would get so frustrated that I wanted to give up on following the Lord because I thought it was too hard. Besides, I didn't understand how God could take a human being, set them apart, and make them holy. I thought as soon as we accepted Christ, we were immediately transformed so in turn, sanctification became difficult for me to grasp. Now I know that transformation is a process with the help of the Holy Spirit, not an overnight change.

Transformation is the position of being transformed into the likeness of Christ (Ephesians 4:22-24) and being conformed to the image of Christ.

I realized that to be transformed is a position where Christ Himself transforms me to be conformed to look like Him. So, in the process of being sanctified, you are going from being conformed to the world's pattern of life to being conformed to the image of Christ, and that is not an easy season to be in. It's what I will call the "S Season."

"The S Season"

Therefore, if anyone cleanses himself from what is dishonorable, he will be a vessel for honorable use, set apart as holy, useful to the master of the house, ready for every good work.
1 Timothy 2:21

What is your biggest distraction when it is time to spend time with God? For me, social media and TV were my distractions. I would say that I was going to spend time with God, but I'd get caught up in watching my favorite shows or scrolling down my timeline. Social networks and television are not dishonorable, but there were things in my life that were, and social networking and TV were distracting me from focus. So, I had to temporarily lay those two aside, spend time with God, and allow Him to form the fruits of the spirit inside of me.

This season of sanctification was the most difficult season for me because there was so much flesh, I had to die to in order to be conformed to His image. As I am writing this section, God has been convicting me to die to certain things. Some things may seem simple,
 but I still need the Holy Spirit's strength to kill them. Yes, I made the decision to abstain, not drink, not curse; you know ... the obvious things, but what about the subtle things: Selfishness, rebellion, envy, and bad spiritual discipline?

It wasn't always fun for me to watch Christian teachings instead of the new episode of my favorite TV show or reading the Bible longer than I read my timeline, but I had to trade everything that would usually be a distraction in for the Word of God, prayer, and obedience.

Because I laid aside my distractions for a while and spent that time in the Word of God, I not only heard the Holy Spirit, but I had the strength of the Holy Spirit to help me do things I wouldn't normally do.

When you are going through the sanctification process the enemy will tempt you to give up. This is a tough position but keep the faith that God is going to complete in you what He started in due season. I realized that although this season didn't feel good, it is a season God uses for the ultimate benefit of His children.

I was reading Ephesians 4:27 and that verse stood out to me the most because it said, "Give no opportunity to the devil." That was referring to anger and strife, but I applied that Scripture to that season of sanctification. During your time of being set apart, the enemy may try to plant thoughts in your mind such as: "What's the point of this?" or my favorite line, "I didn't ask for this."

I remember crying out to God saying, "God, this is not fair!" but the whole time, He was molding me. To this day, I see the product of what He was doing back then when I was complaining. If you are young, it may not feel good, because there is so much pressure when you are young. I used to feel as if from ages 20–22, my life was wasted. I couldn't live like I used to, and it bothered me that I couldn't. But what better investment in the rest of your life than being set apart for Christ Himself at a young age? What an honor to be an adopted heir at 15, 18, 20, or 25 years old and being set apart by God Himself. Always remember that sanctification is what brings transformation, which is a process.

What is sanctification?

_____
_____
_____
_____

Read: I Timothy 2:21. What does this scripture mean to me?

_____
_____
_____
_____

What are some of my biggest distractions that keep me from spending time with God?

_____
_____
_____
_____

Conclusion

Do I know my worth?

Do I understand that no one should be allowed to devalue what God sees as priceless?

Will I save myself for the person that has made the covenant of marriage before me and God?

There was a time when I answered those three questions with no by my actions. Maybe it was because the lifestyle of the people I chose as my role models encouraged an ungodly lifestyle. Maybe it was because I was ignorant to the effects my decision would have on me. Whatever the reason I have gone through many unnecessary heartaches that could have been avoided if I would have denied my fleshly desires. Yeah, I messed up, but my previous answers to those three questions no longer matter. What matters is that I depend on the Holy Spirit to assist me in living a life pleasing to the Lord from now on. I know that Jesus loves me more than any person on this earth could ever love me and He wants to see me whole and righteous living in Him.

Will I allow the Lord to restore me?

Will I allow condemnation or guilt to destroy me?

Will I allow the past to keep me from the love of God and His restoration?

No matter what we have done or what was done to us, being born again means that we have a new chance and a new opportunity to be made new and the past has no relevance.

You are valuable. You are worth it. God has a special purpose for your life. There are hidden talents and not-so-hidden talents that the Lord has given you Jesus is so much more wonderful and amazing than we can ever imagine and having a relationship with Him is the source of my peace and joy. I have only been walking with Him for three years, but He still amazes me daily. I am not trying to create false advertisements because don't get me wrong, this walk is HARD and we have an enemy but the rewards are greater and eternal.

Allow Jesus to show you His love. Ask Jesus to show you who He is and seek His face. Give him a chance, and you won't be able to resist loving Him back.

Thank you for taking the time to read this book. I encourage you to stay close to Christ and watch Him begin to transform your life.

—Ronnesha

Enjoyed the book?

- Feel free to leave your review of this book on **Amazon.com.** I would love to hear your thoughts.

- Pass your copy to someone else you think would benefit from it.

About The Author

Ronnesha Butler is the author of First Comes Love, Then Comes Marriage I & II. She resides in Tennessee with her family and in her free time, she loves cooking, reading, road trips, spending time in the smoky mountains, and quality time with family. She is the author of multiple books including a future novel that is in the works.

She blogs at **Ronneshasjournal.com**

Made in the USA
Columbia, SC
27 September 2023